AF414569

*Some Methods to Solve Group Decision Problems*
Dr. Zoïnabo Savadogo

**CIP a Camerei Naționale a Cărții**

**Savadogo, Zoïnabo.**

Some Methods to Solve Group Decision Problems / Zoïnabo Savadogo. – Chișinău : Generis Publishing, 2020 (Print on demand). – 53 p. : tab.

Referințe bibliogr. la sfârșitul cap.

ISBN 978-9975-154-40-6.

519.816

S 28


Cover image: www.pixabay.com

Generis Publishing
Online orders: www.generis-publishing.com
Orders by email: info@generis-publishing.com

# TABLE OF CONTENTS

# CHAPTER I

# ON NEW AGGREGATION FUNCTIONS OF ADDITIVE VALUE WITHIN THE FRAMEWORK OF THE GROUP DECISION

# ABSTRACT

An average is a value representing a set of data. The main averages are: the arithmetic mean, the geometric mean and the harmonic mean. Some decisions often depend on several contradictory criteria and also on several decision-makers. This is of great importance to group decision support. The dynamics of group aggregation of individual decisions has been a matter of central importance in the theory of decision [12]. There are many problem solving methods that are part of the group decision, but many of them are difficult to use and do not allow to obtain a choice of consensus. It is clear that the arithmetic mean is the one that comes most often in many aggregation functions. In this paper, we use this average to develop a collective aggregation function called the MACASP method.

We also use the harmonic mean for the implementation of another function of collective aggregation, the Lon-Zo method.

Since there is already in the literature a collective aggregation method based on the Electre I method, we make a digital application of these two aggregation functions and carry comparison between the Electre I method, Lon-Zo and MACASP methods.

We find that our two aggregation functions give satisfactory results and are easier to use.

**Keywords and phrases:** *group decision, harmonic mean, Electre I method, arithmetic average, Lon-Zo method, MACASP method.*

# 1. Introduction

Decision-making occurs in any living organism [7]. Deciding is a complex task which sometimes requires the contribution of a third person. Most often we hesitate to take a decision for fear of being wrong. Given the great complexity of decision-making problems, an individual or a group of individuals most often uses outside help to take a decision [13]. Decisions lead to happy or unhappy outcomes; they are subject of regret or satisfaction, and lead to progress or regressions [10]. Most decisions depend on several criteria often conflicting and also on several decision-makers. Multicriteria decision support is a new world of concepts, approaches, models and methods that help the manager (the decision-maker) to describe, evaluate, arrange, choose or reject a set of actions that may be exercised on candidates, products or projects [7].

The group decision is important in any society.

For instance, many decisions are taken at the level of parliamentary laws, in companies, in organizations, etc. Thus, according to Khélifa [3], the group decision fits into two decision-making contexts: first the political context where election decisions and the adoption of laws make calls for voting procedures, next the economic context where decisions are made from individual preferences represented by individual utility functions (also called *partial*) that are aggregated into a collective utility function.

These utility functions are also known as aggregation functions that are conceived through mathematical formulas and whose application allows to determine a choice consensus among several actions.

In the literature, there are a large number of collective aggregation functions, but most often, the application of some of them does not lead to a compromise result. According to Marichal [5], aggregation functions are generally defined and used to combine and summarize multiple numeric values into only one so that the result aggregation takes into account, in a prescribed manner, all individual values. In this work, we will propose two new collective aggregation functions, the Lon-Zo and MACASP methods and we will make a comparison between these methods and the extension from the Electre I method for the group decision that already exists in the literature.

## 2. Presentation of the Harmonic Mean Applied to the Group Decision: the Lon-Zo Method

In this whole part, $w^k_j$ represents the weight assigned to the criterion $j$ by the decision-maker $k$.

Consider the harmonic mean $\overline{x_h}$ of $n$ values $x_i$ next:

$$\overline{x_h} = \frac{n}{\sum_{i=1}^{n}\frac{1}{x_i}}. \tag{2.1}$$

Let us note:

(a) $N$ is the number of decision-makers and $D$ is the set; $D = \{d_1, d_2, ..., d_N\}$;

(b) $m$ is the number of criteria whose set of indices is $\{1, 2, ..., m\}$;

(c) $M$ is the number of shares and their set $A = \{a_1, a_2, ..., a_M\}$.

Note $G_k$ function aggregation additive value for the decision-maker $d_k$. Suppose that the set of actions chosen by all the decision-makers according to each $G_k$ is $\{a_1, a_2, ..., a_k\}$, $k \leq N$.

The collective aggregation function based on the harmonic mean, called the *Lon-Zo method* (*Longin-Zoïnabo*) is defined as follows:

$$U_{(a_i)} = \frac{N}{\sum_{k=1}^{N}\frac{1}{G_k(a_i)}}. \tag{2.2}$$

with

$$G_k(a_i) = \sum_{j=1}^{j=m} w^k_j g^k_j(a_i); \quad i = 1, ..., M; j = 1, ..., m. \tag{2.3}$$

## 3. Applying the Arithmetic mean to the Group Decision: the MACASP Method

Considering $n$ values $x_i$, the arithmetic mean of these $n$ values is given by:

$$\overline{x} = \frac{\sum_{i=1}^{i=n} x_i}{n}. \tag{3.1}$$

We assume $M \geq N$. Note $G_i$ the additive value aggregation function for the decision-maker $d_k$. It is assumed that the set of actions chosen by all the decision-makers according to each $G_i$ is $\{a_1, a_2, ..., a_k\}$; $k \leq N$. We will consider the following arithmetic mean:

$$U_j\ (a_i) = \sum_{i=1}^{N} G_j\ (a_i)/N; \quad i = 1, ..., N;\ \ j = 1, ..., m; \ (3.2)$$

$$G_k\ (a_i) = \sum_{j=1}^{j=m} w_j^{\,k} g_j^{\,k}\ (a_i). \tag{3.3}$$

The collective aggregation function based on the arithmetic mean called *MACASP* (*Modèle d'Agrégation Collective à l'Aide de la Somme Pondérée* ), denoted by $U$ is defined as

$$U\ (a_i) = \sum_{k=1}^{k=N} G_k\ (a_i)/N. \tag{3.4}$$

and

$$U(a_i) = \sum_{k=1}^{k=N} \sum_{j=1}^{j=m} w_j^{\,k} g_j^{\,k}\ (a_i)/N. \tag{3.5}$$

$$U(a_i) = \sum_{j=1}^{j=m} \sum_{k=1}^{k=N} w_j^{\,k} g_j^{\,k}\ (a_i)/N \tag{3.6}$$

After determining the aggregation function, we can then assign an overall score to each action. So we will organize the actions. To better explain our methods and highlight their simplicity, we perform numerical experiments in the next section.

## 4. Digital Experiences

Note that these numerical experiments will allow us to make a comparison.

### 4.1. Example 1

This example is from [2] and [6].

### 4.1.1. The subject

The problem is to find the best product of the set, $A = \{$Product 1, Product 2, Product 3, Product 4$\}$, all actions.

The set of criteria is $F = \{C_1, C_2, C_3, C_4, C_5\}$. With $C_1$: production price (CHF/liter), $C_2$: life of hinge (years), $C_3$: harmful of paint (very little, harmful, very harmful), $C_4$: drying time and $C_5$: smell of paint (not strong, medium, strong, very strong). Data are provided by the decision-makers (or assigned to the criteria) in the form of notes. The extent of the rating scales may differ from one decision-maker to another, and each of the criteria may be assigned as a weighting factor. The result obtained is a distribution on set $A$ of actions (products), one or more outperforming the others. The principle is as follows: the solution that outclasses others must be accepted by as many people as possible, and should not be rejected too clearly, even by only one of them. Each decision-maker builds the matrix of judgment.

**Table 1.** Judgments matrix of $D_1$ (Decision-maker 1)

|               | Price | Lifetime | Odor | Drying | Harmfulness |
|---------------|-------|----------|------|--------|-------------|
| **Minimum scale** | 0 | 0 | 0 | 0 | 0 |
| **Maximum scale** | 10 | 10 | 10 | 10 | 10 |
| **Weight**    | 6 | 3 | 2 | 4 | 3 |
| **Product 1** | 6 | 5 | 2 | 4 | 5 |
| **Product 2** | 5 | 6 | 3 | 3 | 4 |
| **Product 3** | 7 | 5 | 4 | 6 | 3 |
| **Product 4** | 6 | 4 | 5 | 3 | 6 |

Judgments matrix of $D_2$ (Decision-maker 2)

|               | Price | Lifetime | Odor | Drying | Harmfulness |
|---------------|-------|----------|------|--------|-------------|
| **Minimum scale** | 0 | 0 | 0 | 0 | 0 |
| **Maximum scale** | 10 | 10 | 10 | 10 | 10 |
| **Weight**    | 7 | 5 | 3 | 3 | 4 |
| **Product 1** | 7 | 6 | 2 | 3 | 3 |
| **Product 2** | 6 | 5 | 2 | 5 | 3 |
| **Product 3** | 5 | 7 | 3 | 6 | 4 |
| **Product 4** | 5 | 4 | 4 | 4 | 3 |

Judgments matrix of $D_3$ (Decision-maker 3)

|               | Price | Lifetime | Odor | Drying | Harmfulness |
|---------------|-------|----------|------|--------|-------------|
| **Minimum scale** | 0 | 0 | 0 | 0 | 0 |
| **Maximum scale** | 10 | 10 | 10 | 10 | 10 |
| **Weight**    | 6 | 4 | 2 | 3 | 3 |
| **Product 1** | 6 | 5 | 2 | 4 | 4 |
| **Product 2** | 7 | 6 | 3 | 5 | 3 |
| **Product 3** | 6 | 5 | 4 | 3 | 5 |
| **Product 4** | 5 | 4 | 3 | 6 | 4 |

### 4.1.2. Resolution by the Lon-Zo method

Using this example with the Lon-Zo method, we obtain the following table:

| | $\sum_{j=1}^{j=5} w_j^1\, g_j^1(a_i)$ | $\sum_{j=1}^{j=5} w_j^2\, g_j^2(a_i)$ | $\sum_{j=1}^{j=5} w_j^3\, g_j^3(a_i)$ | $U(a_i) = \dfrac{3}{\sum_{k=1}^{3} G_k(a_i)}$ |
|---|---|---|---|---|
| **Product 1** | 86 | 106 | 84 | 91.00 |
| **Product 2** | 78 | 100 | 96 | 90.26 |
| **Product 3** | 98 | 113 | 88 | 98.63 |
| **Product 4** | 88 | 91 | 82 | 86.83 |

Thus, the overall scores of the actions are:

| | |
|---|---|
| **Product 1** | 91.00 |
| **Product 2** | 90.26 |
| **Product 3** | 98.63 |
| **Product 4** | 86.83 |

By this method, we find that Product 3 is the best.

### 4.1.3. Resolution by MACASP

| | $\sum_{k=1}^{3} w_1^k g_1^k(a_i)$ | $\sum_{k=1}^{3} w_2^k g_2^k(a_i)$ | $\sum_{k=1}^{3} w_3^k g_3^k(a_i)$ | $\sum_{k=1}^{3} w_4^k g_4^k(a_i)$ | $\sum_{k=1}^{3} w_5^k g_5^k(a_i)$ | $\dfrac{\sum_{j=1}^{5}\sum_{k=1}^{3} w_j^k\, g_j^k(a_i)}{N}$ |
|---|---|---|---|---|---|---|
| **P1** | 121 | 65 | 14 | 37 | 39 | 276/3 |
| **P2** | 114 | 67 | 18 | 42 | 33 | 274/3 |
| **P3** | 113 | 70 | 25 | 51 | 40 | 299/3 |
| **P4** | 101 | 48 | 28 | 42 | 42 | 261/3 |

**P1** Product 1; **P2** Product 2; **P3** Product 3; **P4** Product 4

The table shows that product 3 is the best compared to other products.

### 4.1.4. Comparison

For this first example, we see that the Lon-Zo and MACASP methods give the same result: Product 3 is the best. In addition, the products are arranged in the same order by each of these methods.

At the level of the literature, the extension of the Electre I method for the group decision has found also that Product 3 is the best.

### 4.2. Example 2

This example is from [1] and [6].

## 4.2.1. The subject

This problem involves choosing a partner from the following set:

$A$ = {Nippon paint KK, Courtaulds coatings, Kansai paint, international paint, US sec. of navy}. The set of criteria is $F$ = {$C_1$, $C_2$, $C_3$, $C_4$} with
$C_1$ : Product quality (good, fair, bad),
$C_2$ : Technology (good, average, bad),
$C_3$ : Cost (Francs),
$C_4$ : Time.

A common preference scale for the four criteria was selected. This choice facilitates the assignment of the importance values (or weights) associated with the criteria. A partner with an average price is preferred.

Choosing a common preference scale greatly facilitates the assignment weights to the criteria. Indeed change a preference scale associated with a criterion requires to change the weight value of this criterion to have some kind of compensation. The data are provided by the decision-makers (or assigned to the criteria) in the form of notes. The extent of the rating scales may differ from one decision-maker to another, and each ratings (or criteria) may be assigned as a weighting factor. The result obtained is a breakdown on set $A$ of shares (companies), one or several outclassing others. The principle is as follows: the solution that outclasses should be accepted by as many people as possible, and should not be rejected too clearly, even by only one of them. Every decision-maker builds the judgment matrix.

Matrix of judgments of $D_1$

|  | Product quality | Technology | Time | Cost |
|---|---|---|---|---|
| Minimum scale | 0 | 0 | 0 | 0 |
| Maximum scale | 10 | 10 | 10 | 10 |
| Weight | 3 | 4 | 3 | 5 |
| Nippon paint KK | 6 | 8 | 9 | 4 |
| Courtaulds coatins | 5 | 5 | 6 | 7 |
| International paint | 7 | 6 | 8 | 4 |
| Kansai paint | 6 | 8 | 4 | 7 |
| US sec. of navy | 5 | 4 | 7 | 6 |

Matrix of judgments of $D_2$

|                      | Product quality | Technology | Time | Cost |
|----------------------|-----------------|------------|------|------|
| Minimum scale        | 0               | 0          | 0    | 0    |
| Maximum scale        | 10              | 10         | 10   | 10   |
| Weight               | 4               | 3          | 2    | 5    |
| Nippon paint KK      | 7               | 5          | 3    | 8    |
| Courtaulds coatins   | 3               | 6          | 8    | 4    |
| International paint  | 6               | 8          | 4    | 3    |
| Kansai paint         | 5               | 4          | 6    | 7    |
| US sec. of navy      | 2               | 3          | 7    | 5    |

Matrix of judgments of $D_3$

|                      | Product quality | Technology | Time | Cost |
|----------------------|-----------------|------------|------|------|
| Minimum scale        | 0               | 0          | 0    | 0    |
| Maximum scale        | 10              | 10         | 10   | 10   |
| Weight               | 4               | 5          | 3    | 5    |
| Nippon paint KK      | 8               | 3          | 6    | 7    |
| Courtaulds coatins   | 6               | 5          | 7    | 3    |
| International paint  | 5               | 8          | 4    | 2    |
| Kansai paint         | 4               | 7          | 3    | 6    |
| US sec. of navy      | 7               | 6          | 5    | 8    |

## 4.2.2. Resolution by the Lon-Zo method

We will again use this example with our method.

|                      | $\sum_{j=1}^{j=4} w_j^1 g_j^1(a_i)$ | $\sum_{j=1}^{j=4} w_j^2 g_j^2(a_i)$ | $\sum_{j=1}^{j=4} w_j^3 g_j^3(a_i)$ | $\dfrac{3}{\sum_{k=1}^{3} \frac{1}{G_k(a_i)}}$ |
|----------------------|------|------|------|--------|
| Nippon paint KK      | 97   | 89   | 100  | 95.10  |
| Courtaulds coatins   | 85   | 66   | 85   | 77.55  |
| International paint  | 89   | 71   | 82   | 79.96  |
| Kansai paint         | 97   | 79   | 90   | 88.03  |
| US sec. of navy      | 82   | 56   | 113  | 77.11  |

Thus, the overall scores of the actions are:

|                      |        |
|----------------------|--------|
| Nippon paint KK      | 95.10  |
| Courtaulds coatins   | 77.55  |
| International paint  | 79.96  |
| Kansai paint         | 88.03  |
| US sec. of navy      | 77.11  |

11

By this method, we find that Nippon paint is the best partner.

## 4.2.3. Resolution by the MACASP method

| | $\sum_{k=1}^{3} w_1^k g_1^k(a_i)$ | $\sum_{k=1}^{3} w_2^k g_2^k(a_i)$ | $\sum_{k=1}^{3} w_3^k g_3^k(a_i)$ | $\sum_{k=1}^{3} w_4^k g_4^k(a_i)$ | $\dfrac{\sum_{j=1}^{4}\sum_{k=1}^{3} w_j^k g_j^k(a_i)}{N}$ |
|---|---|---|---|---|---|
| Nippon paint KK | 78 | 62 | 51 | 95 | 286/3 |
| Courtaulds coatins | 48 | 63 | 55 | 70 | 236/3 |
| International paint | 65 | 88 | 44 | 45 | 242/3 |
| Kansai paint | 54 | 79 | 33 | 100 | 266/3 |
| US sec. of navy | 51 | 55 | 50 | 95 | 251/3 |

We also see that Nippon paint is the most interesting partner.

## 4.2.4. Comparison

We also see that Nippon paint is the most interesting partner through each of these methods. Similarly, the extension of the Electre I method for decision group finds the same result.

## 5. Conclusion

The complexity and importance of management problems encountered in many organizations sometimes lead to the search for a "scientific preparation" for decisions that is called a decision aid [8]. Decision support is done through aggregation methods. There is a long list of aggregation methods in the literature, but many of them are based on the arithmetic mean.

According to Haccoun and Cousineau, the arithmetic mean is sometimes the most useful statistic and the most frequently used, both in scientific and professional life, as well as in daily life. According to the same source, despite the disadvantages of the average, it is the quintessential estimate of the central tendency of a sample and makes the least mistakes when used to "predict" each value of the distribution [11]. It seems that arithmetic mean has several advantages but has a major drawback which is the fact that it is sensitive to extreme values and to circumvent it, one could move towards a reduced average. Lon-Zo and MACASP methods are problems of storage. These answer the question of how to arrange candidates for competition in descending order of merit [14]. This storage is done due to the global scores generated by the collective aggregation function obtained by the different functions of additive value.

Numerical examples have shown that the results provided by Electre I do not differ significantly from those generated by Lon-Zo and MACASP. The extension of the Electre I method generates many calculations as one can see through its description in [4] and also its application in [1]. On the other hand, Lon-Zo and MACASP methods are easier to use. The aggregation functions Lon-Zo and MACASP therefore seem better indicated than Electre I for solve multi-criteria problems.

# REFERENCES

**[1]** R. Ginting, Intégration du système d'aide multicritère et du système d'intélligence économique dans l'ère concurrentielle, 11/01/2000 application dans le choix de partenaires en Indonésie, Thèse, Université de droit et des Sciences d'Aix-Marseille.

**[2]** Rasmi Ginting and Henri Dou, L'approche multidécideur multicritère d'aide à la décision, cedex 20, France.

**[3]** Slim Ben Khélifa, L'aide multicritère à la décision de groupe: l'approche du surclassement de synthèse, Thèse, Université Laval, Quebec, 1998.

**[4]** Adel Hatami-Marbini and Madjid Tavana, An extension of the Electre I method for group decision-making under a fuzzy environment, Omega 39 (2011), 373-386.

**[5]** Jean-Luc Marichal, Fonctions d'agrégation pour la décision, Brigham Young University, 2003.

**[6]** Zoïnabo Savadogo, Ruffin-Benoît M. Ngoie and Berthold E.-L. Ulungu and Blaise Somé, An aggregation function to solve multicriteria ranking problem involving several decision makers, International Journal of Applied Mathematical Research 3(4) (2014), 511-517.

**[7]** Taibi Boumedyen, L'analyse multicritère comme outil d'aide à la décision: Aplication de la méthode promethee, mémoire, 209-2010, Université Abou-Bekr-Belkaid Tlemcen.

**[8]** D. Bouyssou, Th. Marchant and P. Perny, Théorie du choix social et aide multicritère à la décision, Mai 2002 - révsion 13 Octobre 2005.

**[9]** Slim Ben Khélifa, L'Aide multicritère à la décision de groupe: L'approche du surclassement de synthèse, Thèse, Université Laval, 1998.

**[10]** P. Fixmer, Brassac: La décision collective comme processus de construction de sens, C. Bonardi, N. Grégori, J.-Y Menard and N. Roussiau, eds., Psychologie Sociale Appliquée, Emploi, travail, resources humaines, Paris, 2004, pp. 111-118.

[11]  Robert R. Haccoun and Denis Cousineau, Statistiques: concepts et applications, les presses de l'Université de Montréal, 2007.

[12]  Dorit S. Hochbaum and Asaf Levin, Methodologies and algorithms for group-rankings decision, Management Science 52(9) (2006), 1394-1408.

[13]  Belacel Nabil, Méthodes de classification multicritère: méthodo logie et applications à l'aide au diagnostic médical, Thèse, Université Libre de Bruxelles, 1999-2000.

[14]  A. Carlos and Bana E. Costa, Les problématiques de l'aide à la décision: vers l'enrichissement de la trilogie choix-tri-rangement, Revue française d'automatique, d'informatique et de recherche opérationnelle, Recherché Opérationnelle 30 (1996), 191-216.

# CHAPTER II

# NEW METRIC PROCEDURE BASED ON APPROVAL VOTING

# ACKNOWLEDGEMENT

I acknowledge A Project Supported by Scientific Research Fund of Hunan Provincial Education Department (Grant No: 19C0860).

# ABSTRACT

Voting methods consist in transforming individual preferences into a collective preference.

But most of the time we find that many methods do not allow for consensus and this often leads to post-election conflicts. So, in this work, we have proposed a new voting method based on approval voting that is well appreciated in the literature by some authors and over a distance that will tend towards a general interest for all voters.

This method is also called metric procedure.

Since this method is combined with approval voting and a distance that minimizes the number of disagreements among voters, it generates good properties.

The method has been tested on two examples and the results are verified by a comparative study with the method of Kemeny and Snell. The results on these problems allowed to show the performance of our method.

# 1. Introduction

According to [6], the main goal of social choice theory is to answer the question how to aggregate individual preferences into a collective preference? And the answer leads us obviously to the study of the voting procedures.

According to [4], the vote consists to look for a mechanism (electoral system or aggregation method) to "reasonably" aggregate the opinions expressed in an election by several voters on various candidates in order to determine a winner (the elected candidate) or to order in order of preference amongst the various candidates.

In the book [8], Arrow defines voting as a function to synthesize individual preferences into a collective preference. This study was strongly dominated by the ordinal approach, in [11] and [2], the authors propose to move to the cardinal approach.

In recent years, several authors have been interested in the cardinal theory of social choice [10].

In this, last approach is the vote by approval.

Many voting methods exist in the literature.

But the aggregation of individual preferences into collective preferences encounters difficulties and generates many paradoxes [6].

And according to impossibility theorems, no method fulfills all the desirable properties. Most of them are complex and mostly reflect the choice of voters. With the difficulties encountered in aggregating individual preferences into a collective preference, several authors have tried to propose solutions.

In his essay on the application of analysis to the probability of decisions and the plurality of votes [5], the Marquis of Condorcet shows that the plurality vote, that is, simple majority voting does not always give satisfactory results when voters have to choose between three or more options; a natural attitude is to ask voters to provide richer information than in a single-member system [3].

Similarly, one of the solutions would be to ask the voters to provide richer information than in a uninominal vote [4].

Other authors advocate voting methods based on a distance called metric procedures.

Thus, Kemeny [19] proposed the number of disagreements or inversions as distance between two orders and a Kemeny order is the one that minimizes the sum of disagreements with the orders of all judges and an order of Kemeny can be seen as a best possible compromise between divergent views.

In the interest of reducing the contrasts observed in the voting methods, we opted to contribute to the literature by a voting method based not only on the vote by assent but on a distance that minimizes the disagreements.

The paper is organized as follows. Section 2 presents a review on the literature. In Section 3, we present the new method, the applications are in Section 4, Section 5 presents the performance of both the methods in computation time, and conclusions and future work are given in Section 6.

## 2. Review of the Literature on Metric Procedures

This section is from [7].

In the literature, a lot of metric procedures have been studied:

The method of Kemeny and Snell [14]

It consists to determine a consensual storage from individual storage. More precisely, the structures preferably are of type {>. «}. The consensus is based on a distance function that determines a minimum distance storage of individual storage. This function must verify some axioms as any function of social choice; in particular, a metric, the axiom of neutrality, must ignore the actions (candidates) who occupy the same positions in the individual storages since. a priori. a consensus emerges from these actions. The last axiom requires that a distance is positive and is at least equal to unit. In addition to providing a set of conditions that a distance function must necessarily check. these axioms guarantee the existence and uniqueness of such a function when the metric $\|\cdot\|_1$ is used. We represent the individual storage in matrix form

$$M^{(t)} = \left[m_{ik}^{(t)}\right]; t \in T \text{ with } m_{ir}^t = \begin{cases} 1 & if \quad x_i \quad \succ^t x_k \\ 1/2 & if \quad x_i \quad \simeq^t x_k. \\ 0 & if \quad x_k \quad \succ^t x_j \end{cases}$$

Aggregation consists to determine a matrix $B = [b_{ik}]$ transitive which is the most representative of matrices $M^t = [m_{ik}^t]$, $t \in T$. T is the set of decision-makers (voters). Consensus is achieved by minimizing the number of disagreements between B and M$^t$:

$$min\left\{\sum_{t=1}^{s}\sum_{i=1}^{m}\sum_{k=1}^{m}|b_{ik} - m_{ik}^t| : B \in WO\right\} = min\left\{\sum_{t=l}^{s} \delta_{KS}(B, M^t) : B \in WO\right\},$$

where $WO$ is the set of complete preorders.

## 2.2 Blin's method

Blin [16] proposed a model that consists to determine from individual storage linear (relations of strict order) a linear consensual arrangement. The storage is represented in matrix form: $P^t = [p_{ir}^t], t \in T$ with

$$p_{ir}^t = \begin{cases} 1 & \text{if } x_i \text{ occupies the rank } r \in \left\{1, \frac{3}{2}, m-1, m-\frac{1}{2}, m\right\} \\ 0 & \text{otherwise.} \end{cases}$$

This representation is not limited to strict relationships, it can be extended to total preorders (Armstrong et al. [15]). Blin's [16] approach consists to determine a consensual arrangement $Q = [q_{it}]$ showing the minimum of disagreements with the matrices $P^t = [p_{ir}^t]$, $t \in T$ which amounts to solving:

$$min\left\{\sum_{t=1}^{s}\sum_{i=1}^{m}\sum_{k=1}^{m}|q_{ik} - p_{ik}^t| : Q \in SO\right\} = min\left\{\sum_{t-1}^{s}\delta_{BL}(Q, P^t) : Q \in SO\right\},$$

where $SO$ is the set of strict order relations, $s$ is the number of decision makers, and m is the number of candidates. The problem is transformed into an assignment problem whose optimal solution is obtained by application of a classical resolution algorithm (Hungarian method).

## 2.3 The method of Barthelemy [17]

Barthelemy [17] presented an axiomatization of the distance of the symmetrical difference: $\delta(H, S) = |H \cup S| - |H \cap S|$, $H$ and S being two binary relations.

Barthelemy et al. [18] proposed two heuristics for determining a relation of order strict median obtained from a profile of preferences constituted by order relations strict as well as an algorithm of the type << *Branch - and - bound* >> to generate all orders medians from a preference profile consisting of strict order relationships.

## 2.4 The method of the Cook and Seiford model [20]

The Cook and Seiford model [20] calculates the distance between two storage units by making the difference between the ranks of the shares. The consensus storage $R^* = (r_1^*, \dots, r_m^*)$ is the one that minimizes the gaps

$$|r_i^t - r_i^*|, t \in T : min\left\{\sum_{t=1}^{s}\sum_{i=1}^{m}|r_i^t - r_i^*| : (R^* \in SO) \vee (R^* \in WO)\right\}.$$

These different codings are to solve problems of minimum distance, because they are problems with integer variables, so the resolution is more complicated than those with continuous variables, there including constraints on transitivity.

In addition to using the metric $L_1$, we can also use the metric $L_2$ whose formulation is

$$min\left\{\sum_{t=1}^{s}\sum_{i=1}^{m}\sum_{k=1}^{m}(b_{ik} - m_{ik}^{t})^2 : B \in SO\right\}$$

The algorithms for solving previous minimization problems that fall under the mathematical programming are likely to offer multiple solutions. It belongs to the decision makers to find a solution of consensus.

## 2.5 New metric procedure of multi-decisions makers choice

Savadogo et al. [9] have also contributed in the literature relating to metric procedures with their method entitled "New metric procedure of multi-decisions makers choice".

In order to find a method that reflects the sincere group selection, they were inspired by one of the systems that encourages mostly the revelation of sincere preferences. This is the approval voting but with a preference multichoices with four levels of indifference. The idea is to rank candidates with a possibility to have more than two candidates in the same class.

The coding of this method is as follows:

$$M^{(t)} = \left[m_{ir}^{(t)}\right] ; t \in T$$

with

$$m_{ir}^{t} = \begin{cases} 1 & \text{if } c_i \text{ is at 1st choice} \\ 1/2 & \text{if } c_i \text{ is at 2nd choice} \\ 0 & \text{if } c_i \text{ is at 3rd choice} \\ -1/2 & \text{if } c_i \text{ is at 4th choice} \\ -1 & \text{else.} \end{cases}$$

Four more information, the interested reader can refer to the following document [9].

# 3. New Voting Method

The new method is also called NVMBAV (new voting method based on approval voting).

## 3.1 Codification

Let us consider $E$ as a set of $m$ candidates for an election, with $m \geq 2$ and a set of $s$ voters with $s \geq 2$. So, the method is as follows: Each of the $s$ voters uses elements of $P(E)$ disjointed and whose meeting gives $E$, according to the following order: choice 1, choice 2, choice 3, choice 4. It assigns each element of each of its subsets, respectively, as the notes

$$\frac{4}{4}, \frac{3}{4}, \frac{2}{4}, \frac{1}{4}.$$

It should be noted here that one could also obtain whole numbered notes, for example, 5, 4, 2, 1 instead of $\frac{4}{4}, \frac{3}{4}, \frac{2}{4}, \frac{1}{4}.$

For example, consider $E = \{c_1, c_2, c_3, c_4, c_5\}$ a set of 5 candidates.

The following table represents the choice of a voter:

| choice 1 | choice 2 | choice 3 | choice 4 |
|---|---|---|---|
| $\{c_2, c_3\}$ | $\{c_1\}$ | $\{c_4\}$ | $\{c_5\}$ |

So, $c_2$ and $c_3$ have each $\frac{4}{4}$; $c_1$ has $\frac{3}{4}$; $c_4$ has $\frac{2}{4}$; and $c_5$ has $\frac{1}{4}$.

Then we divide the candidates into three groups as follows:
- $G_{sup}$ for those who are above average.

- $G_{moy}$ for those who have exactly the average.

- $G_{inf}$ for those who are below average.

## 3.2. Matrix storage of the new methodology

- We represent the individual storages in matrix form

$$A^{(t)} = \left[a_{ik}^{(t)}\right]; t \in T \text{ with } a_{ik}^t = \begin{cases} \frac{3}{4} & \text{if } c_i \in G_{sup} \\ \frac{2}{4} & \text{if } c_i \in G_{sup} \\ \frac{1}{4} & \text{if } c_i \in G_{sup} \\ 0 & \text{else.} \end{cases} \tag{1}$$

The approach is to determine a consensual arrangement $C = [c_{it}]$ showing off the minimum of disagreements with the matrices $A^t = [a_{ik}^t]$, $t \in T$, which amounts to solving:

$$min\left\{\sum_{t=1}^{s}\sum_{i=1}^{m}\sum_{k=1}^{m}|c_{ik} - a_{ik}^t| : C \in SO\right\}, (2)$$

where

• $SO$ is the set of relations of strict order;

• s is the number of decision makers;

• $m$ the number of candidates.

It should be noted that the codification of our method does not depend on the way in which the notes were distributed to the candidates.

## 4. Applications

### 4.1 Example 1

Consider five candidates and 3 voters whose choices are:

$R^{(1)} =$

| choice 1 | choice 2 | choice 3 | choice 4 |
|---|---|---|---|
| $\{c_2, c_3\}$ | $\{c_1\}$ | $\{c_4\}$ | $\{c_5\}$ |

$R^{(2)} =$

| choice 1 | choice 2 | choice 3 | choice 4 |
|---|---|---|---|
| $\{c_2\}$ | $\{c_1\}$ | $\{c_4\}$ | $\{c_3, c_5\}$ |

$R^{(3)} =$

| choice 1 | choice 2 | choice 3 | choice 4 |
|---|---|---|---|
| $\{c_1\}$ | $\{c_3\}$ | $\{c_2, c_4\}$ | $\{c_5\}$ |

Thus, by $R^{(1)}$, the notes are:

| $c_1$ | $c_2$ | $c_3$ | $c_4$ | $c_5$ |
|---|---|---|---|---|
| $\dfrac{3}{4}$ | $\dfrac{4}{4}$ | $\dfrac{4}{4}$ | $\dfrac{2}{4}$ | $\dfrac{1}{4}$ |

The average of the candidates' scores is $\dfrac{14}{20}$, putting all the notes at the same denominator gives the following table:

| $c_1$ | $c_2$ | $c_3$ | $c_4$ | $c_5$ |
|---|---|---|---|---|
| $\dfrac{15}{20}$ | $\dfrac{20}{20}$ | $\dfrac{20}{20}$ | $\dfrac{10}{20}$ | $\dfrac{5}{20}$ |

So, $G_{sup} = \{c_1, c_2, c_3\}$; $G_{moy} = \{\ \}$, $G_{inf} = \{c_4, c_5\}$.

Thus, by $R^{(2)}$, we have the following notes:

| $c_1$ | $c_2$ | $c_3$ | $c_4$ | $c_5$ |
|---|---|---|---|---|
| $\dfrac{3}{4}$ | $\dfrac{4}{4}$ | $\dfrac{1}{4}$ | $\dfrac{2}{4}$ | $\dfrac{1}{4}$ |

The average of the candidates' scores is $\dfrac{12}{20}$, putting all the notes at the same denominator gives the following table:

| $c_1$ | $c_2$ | $c_3$ | $c_4$ | $c_5$ |
|---|---|---|---|---|
| $\dfrac{15}{20}$ | $\dfrac{20}{20}$ | $\dfrac{5}{20}$ | $\dfrac{10}{20}$ | $\dfrac{5}{20}$ |

So, $G_{sup} = \{c_1, c_2\}$; $G_{moy} = \{\ \}$, $G_{inf} = \{c_3, c_4, c_5\}$.

Thus, by $R^{(3)}$, we have the following notes:

| $c_1$ | $c_2$ | $c_3$ | $c_4$ | $c_5$ |
|---|---|---|---|---|
| $\dfrac{4}{4}$ | $\dfrac{2}{4}$ | $\dfrac{3}{4}$ | $\dfrac{2}{4}$ | $\dfrac{1}{4}$ |

The average of the candidates' scores is $\dfrac{11}{20}$, putting all the notes at the same denominator gives the following table:

| $c_1$ | $c_2$ | $c_3$ | $c_4$ | $c_5$ |
|---|---|---|---|---|
| $\dfrac{20}{20}$ | $\dfrac{10}{20}$ | $\dfrac{15}{20}$ | $\dfrac{10}{20}$ | $\dfrac{5}{20}$ |

So, $G_{sup} = \{c_1, c_3\}$; $G_{moy} = \{\ \}$, $G_{inf} = \{c_2, c_4, c_5\}$.

## 4.1.1. Resolution with the new method

The matrices of choice are given by:

$$A^{(1)} = \begin{pmatrix}
 & G_{sup} & G_{moy} & G_{inf} \\
c_1 & \frac{3}{4} & 0 & 0 \\
c_2 & \frac{3}{4} & 0 & 0 \\
c_3 & \frac{3}{4} & 0 & 0 \\
c_4 & 0 & 0 & \frac{1}{4} \\
c_5 & 0 & 0 & \frac{1}{4}
\end{pmatrix}.$$

$$A^2 = \begin{pmatrix}
 & G_{sup} & G_{moy} & G_{inf} \\
c_1 & \frac{3}{4} & 0 & 0 \\
c_2 & \frac{3}{4} & 0 & 0 \\
c_3 & 0 & 0 & \frac{1}{4} \\
c_4 & 0 & 0 & \frac{1}{4} \\
c_5 & 0 & 0 & \frac{1}{4}
\end{pmatrix},$$

$$A^{(3)} = \begin{pmatrix}
 & G_{sup} & G_{moy} & G_{inf} \\
c_1 & \frac{3}{4} & 0 & 0 \\
c_2 & 0 & 0 & \frac{1}{4} \\
c_3 & \frac{3}{4} & 0 & 0 \\
c_4 & 0 & 0 & \frac{1}{4} \\
c_5 & 0 & 0 & \frac{1}{4}
\end{pmatrix}.$$

The results provided by the code are:

• The best choice is

| 1 | 1 | 1 | 0.25 | 0.25 |
|---|---|---|------|------|

The matrix is

$$R^{(1)} = \begin{pmatrix} \frac{3}{4} & 0 & 0 \\ \frac{3}{4} & 0 & 0 \\ \frac{3}{4} & 0 & 0 \\ 0 & 0 & \frac{1}{4} \\ 0 & 0 & \frac{1}{4} \end{pmatrix}.$$

- The minimum of disagreements is 2.

## 4.1.2. Resolution by the method of Kemeny and Snell

With the method of Kemeny and Snell, we obtain:

The best choice is

| 1 | 1 | 1 | 0.5 | 0.25 |
|---|---|---|-----|------|

The storage matrix:

$$\begin{pmatrix} 0 & \frac{1}{1} & \frac{1}{2} & 1 & 1 \\ \frac{1}{2} & 0 & \frac{1}{2} & 1 & 1 \\ \frac{1}{2} & \frac{1}{2} & 0 & 1 & 1 \\ 0 & 0 & 0 & 0 & 1 \\ 0 & 0 & 0 & 0 & 0 \end{pmatrix}.$$

Minimum of disagreements is 12.

## 4.2 Example 2

Consider 5 voters and 4 candidates whose choices are:

$$R^{(1)} = \begin{array}{|c|c|c|c|} \hline \text{choice 1} & \text{choice 2} & \text{choice 3} & \text{choice 4} \\ \{c_2, c_4\} & \{c_1\} & \{c_3\} & \\ \hline \end{array}$$

Thus, by $R^{(1)}$, we have the following notes:

| $c_1$ | $c_2$ | $c_3$ | $c_4$ |
|---|---|---|---|
| $\dfrac{3}{4}$ | $\dfrac{4}{4}$ | $\dfrac{2}{4}$ | $\dfrac{4}{4}$ |

Average $= \dfrac{13}{16}$; $G_{sup} = \{c_2, c_4\}$; $G_{moy} = \{\ \}$; $G_{inf} = \{c_1, c_3\}$.

$$R^{(2)} = \begin{array}{|c|c|c|c|} \hline \text{choice 1} & \text{choice 2} & \text{choice 3} & \text{choice 4} \\ \{c_1\} & \{c_3\} & \{c_4\} & \{c_2\} \\ \hline \end{array}$$

Thus, by $R^{(2)}$, we have the following notes:

| $c_1$ | $c_2$ | $c_3$ | $c_4$ |
|---|---|---|---|
| $\dfrac{4}{4}$ | $\dfrac{1}{4}$ | $\dfrac{3}{4}$ | $\dfrac{2}{4}$ |

Average $= \dfrac{10}{16}$; $G_{sup} = \{c_1, c_3\}$; $G_{moy} = \{\ \}$; $G_{inf} = \{c_2, c_4\}$.

$$R^{(3)} = \begin{array}{|c|c|c|c|} \hline \text{choice 1} & \text{choice 2} & \text{choice 3} & \text{choice 4} \\ \{c_3\} & \{c_1\} & \{c_2, c_4\} & \\ \hline \end{array}$$

Thus, by $R^{(3)}$, we have the following notes:

| $c_1$ | $c_2$ | $c_3$ | $c_4$ |
|---|---|---|---|
| $\dfrac{3}{4}$ | $\dfrac{2}{4}$ | $\dfrac{4}{4}$ | $\dfrac{2}{4}$ |

Average $= \dfrac{11}{16}$; $G_{sup} = \{c_1, c_3\}$; $G_{moy} = \{\ \}$; $G_{inf} = \{c_2, c_4\}$.

$$R^{(4)} = \begin{array}{|c|c|c|c|} \hline \text{choice 1} & \text{choice 2} & \text{choice 3} & \text{choice 4} \\ & \{c_1\} & \{c_2, c_4\} & \{c_3\} \\ \hline \end{array}$$

Thus, by R$^{(4)}$, we have the following notes:

| $c_1$ | $c_2$ | $c_3$ | $c_4$ |
|---|---|---|---|
| $\dfrac{3}{4}$ | $\dfrac{2}{4}$ | $\dfrac{1}{4}$ | $\dfrac{2}{4}$ |

$$\text{Average} = \frac{8}{16}; \; G_{sup} = \{c_1\}; \; G_{moy} = \{c_2, c_4\}; \; G_{inf} = \{c_3\}.$$

$$R^{(5)} = \begin{array}{|c|c|c|c|}
\hline
\text{choice 1} & \text{choice 2} & \text{choice 3} & \text{choice 4} \\
\{c_1\} & \{c_3\} & & \{c_2, c_4\} \\
\hline
\end{array}$$

Thus, by R$^{(5)}$, we have the following notes:

| $c_1$ | $c_2$ | $c_3$ | $c_4$ |
|---|---|---|---|
| $\dfrac{4}{4}$ | $\dfrac{1}{4}$ | $\dfrac{3}{4}$ | $\dfrac{1}{4}$ |

$$\text{Average} = \frac{9}{16}; \; G_{sup} = \{c_1, c_3\}; \; G_{moy} = \{ \; \}; \; G_{inf} = \{c_2, c_4\}.$$

## 4.2.1. Resolution with the new method

The matrices of choice are:

$$A^{(1)} = \begin{array}{c c c c}
 & G_{sup} & G_{moy} & G_{inf} \\
c_1 & 0 & 0 & \frac{1}{4} \\
c_2 & \frac{3}{4} & 0 & 0 \\
c_3 & 0 & 0 & \frac{1}{4} \\
c_4 & \frac{3}{4} & 0 & 0
\end{array},$$

$$A^{(2)} = \begin{pmatrix} & G_{sup} & G_{moy} & G_{inf} \\ c_1 & \frac{3}{4} & 0 & 0 \\ c_2 & 0 & 0 & \frac{1}{4} \\ c_3 & \frac{3}{4} & 0 & 0 \\ c_4 & 0 & 0 & \frac{1}{4} \end{pmatrix},$$

$$A^{(3)} = \begin{pmatrix} & G_{sup} & G_{moy} & G_{inf} \\ c_1 & \frac{3}{4} & 0 & 0 \\ c_2 & 0 & 0 & \frac{1}{4} \\ c_3 & \frac{3}{4} & 0 & 0 \\ c_4 & 0 & 0 & \frac{1}{4} \end{pmatrix},$$

$$A^{(4)} = \begin{pmatrix} & G_{sup} & G_{moy} & G_{inf} \\ c_1 & \frac{3}{4} & 0 & 0 \\ c_2 & 0 & \frac{2}{4} & 0 \\ c_3 & 0 & 0 & \frac{1}{4} \\ c_4 & 0 & \frac{2}{4} & 0 \end{pmatrix},$$

$$A^{(5)} = \begin{pmatrix} & G_{sup} & G_{moy} & G_{inf} \\ c_1 & \frac{3}{4} & 0 & 0 \\ c_2 & 0 & 0 & \frac{1}{4} \\ c_3 & \frac{3}{4} & 0 & 0 \\ c_4 & 0 & 0 & \frac{1}{4} \end{pmatrix}.$$

The best choice is

| 1 | 0.25 | 1 | 0.25 |
|---|---|---|---|

The matrix is

$$\begin{pmatrix} \frac{3}{4} & 0 & 0 \\ 0 & 0 & \frac{1}{4} \\ \frac{3}{4} & 0 & 0 \\ 0 & 0 & \frac{1}{4} \end{pmatrix}.$$

The minimum of disagreements is 6.5.

### 4.2.2 Resolution by the method of Kemeny and Snell

With the method of Kemeny and Snell, we obtain:

- Best choice

| 1 | 0.25 | 0.5 | 0.25 |
|---|------|-----|------|

- Its storage matrix:

$$\begin{pmatrix} 0 & 1 & 1 & 1 \\ 0 & 0 & 0 & \dfrac{1}{1} \\ 0 & 1 & 0 & 1 \\ 0 & \dfrac{1}{2} & 0 & 0 \end{pmatrix}.$$

- Minimum of disagreements: 15.

## 4. Performance of Both the Methods in Computation Time

To measure the performance of both the methods in terms of computation time, we ran the simulation 50 times for each example. The characteristics of the computer used are:

Processor: Intel(R) Core (TM) i7-4710MQ CPU @2.50GHz 2.250GHz, RAM: 12GB, Operating System: Windows 10, 64-bit.

The statistical results in second are given in Table 1.

**Table 1.** Computation time

| | Our method | | | | Method of Kemeny and Sell | | | |
|---|---|---|---|---|---|---|---|---|
| | Min | Max | Mean | Std | Min | Max | Mean | Std |
| Example 1 | 0.14 | 0.265 | 0.195 | 0.031 | 0.359 | 0.578 | 0.43 | 0.049 |
| Example 2 | 0.031 | 0.187 | 0.068 | 0.027 | 0.109 | 0.406 | 0.147 | 0.043 |

By observing these results, we see that the new method is faster than the method of Kemeny and Snell. These results show that our method is able to provide very competitive results compared to the method of Kemeny and Snell.

# 5. Conclusion

In this article, we have proposed a new metric procedure. This code has been programmed in Matlab using the Hungarian algorithm. And it has been then tested on two examples. The results obtained were compared with the codification proposed by Kemeny and Snell. The best choices are not exactly the same for both the methods, but both the methods always give the same best candidates. On the other hand, disagreements are more minimized in our approach.

We find that if we have 10000 candidates, with the method of Kemeny and Snell, we will have the matrices of 10000 rows 10000 columns.

While with the new method, regardless of the number of candidates, we only have three columns.

So, the new method generates fewer calculations than the Kemeny and Snell method.

Since the method also uses the vote by approval, it generates good properties. Indeed after [1], majority ballot asks very little information to the elector as he has only the right to appoint a single candidate. The vote by approval requires him to nominate as many candidates as he wishes.

But despite everything, it seems that there is no totally satisfactory voting method.

So, according to [12], the question of the "best" voting system, cannot be more tropical, is indeed a thorny issue.

As a perspective, we intend to apply our approach in solving multicriteria decision support problems.

# REFERENCES

[1] M. Balinski and R. Laraki, Jugement majoritaire vs vote majoritaire (via les presidentielles 2011-2012), Cahier no 2012-37, CNRS, 2012.

[2] A. Baujard and H. Igersheim, Experimentation du vote par note et du vote par approbation lors de l'election presidentielle francaise du 22 avril 2007, Technical Report, Centre D'analyse Strategique, 2007.

[3] P. Blanchenay, Paradoxes de vote et modes de scrutin en france, Master's Thesis, Ecole des Hautes Etudes Commerciales Majeure Economie, 2004.

[4] D. Bouyssou, T. Marchant and P. Perny, Theorie du choix social et aide multicritere a la decision, Working Paper, LAMSADE, 2005.

[5] M. J. A. de Condorcet, Essai sur l'application de l'analyse a la probabilite des decisions rendues a la pluralite des voix, Paris:l'Imprimerie Royale [fascimile edition, 1972], 1785.

[6] S. Durand, Sur quelques paradoxes en theorie du choix social et en decision multicritere, Ph.D. Thesis, Universite Joseph Fourier-Grenoble 1 Sciences et Geographie, 2000.

[7] S. B. Khelifa, L'Aide Multicritere a la Decisionde Groupe: L'approche du surclassemnt de synthese, Ph.D. Thesis, Universite Laval Quebec, 1998.

[8] K. J. Arrow, Social Choice and Individual Values, Wiley, New York, 1951 and 1963.

[9] Z. Savadogo, P. O. F. Ouedraogo, K. Some, O. So, B. Ulungu and B. Some, New metric procedure of multi-decisions makers choice, Far East J. Appl. Math. 95(5) (2016), 329-341.

[10] O. Sicard, Theorie du choix social, une version cardinale de la theorie du choix social, Episode 3, 2016.

[11] H. Smaoui and D. Lepelley, Le systeme de vote a trois niveaux: Etude d'un nouveau mode de scrutin, Revue d'economie Politique 123(6) (2013), 827-850.

[12] J. G. Suitt, A. Guyon, T. Hennion, R. Laraki, X. Starkloff, S. Thibault and B. Favreau, Vers un systeme de vote plus juste, Cahier no 2014-20, CNRS, Septembre 2014.

[13] M. Truchon, Choix social et comites de selection: le cas du patinage artistique, Technical Report, Universite Laval, CIRANO, Novembre 2002.

[14] J. G. Kemeny and L. J. Snell, Preference Ranking: An Axiomatic Approach in Mathematical Models in the Social Sciences, Ginn, New York, 1962, pp. 9-23.

[15] R. D. Armstrong, W. D. Cook and L. M. Seiford, Priority ranking and

consensus formation, Management Science 28 (1982), 638-648.

[16]  J. M. Blin, A linear assignment formulation for the multiattribute decision problem, RAIRO 10 (1976), 21-32.

[17]  J. P. Barthelemy, Caracterisation axiomatiques de la distance de la difference symetrique entre relations binaries, Mathematiques et Sciences Humaines 17 (1979), 85- 113.

[18]  J. P. Barthelemy, A. Guenoche and O. Hudry, Median linear orders: heuristics and branch-and-bo & algorithm, European J. Oper. Res. 42 (1989), 313-325.

[19]  J. G. Kemeny, Mathematics without numbers, Daedalus 88(4) (1959), 577-591.

[20]  W. D. Cook and L. M. Seiford, Priority ranking and consensus formation, Management Science 24 (1978), 1721-1732.

# CHAPTER III

# VOTING METHOD BASED ON AN AVERAGE GAP ASSESSMENT

# ABSTRACT

The theory of social choice is the study of voting methods. In the literature many studies have been conducted for the development of a fair voting system, that is to say a voting method that allows to aggregate the individual preferences in a collective preference representing in the most possible faithfull way individual preferences. Yet some voting methods do not allow to obtain a consensus. So there are a lot of paradoxes in electoral systems and related results in the theory of social choice are also paradoxical. This is the case, for example, with Arrow's theorem showing that no voting method can simultaneously verify a restricted list of properties that are desirable in a democratic political system. That is to mean that the search for a system that makes it possible to reach a consensus remains a concern in the theory of social choice. In this article we have combined various voting methods based on grading, scoring or approving to contribute to literature with a new voting system lling fair properties.

**2010 Mathematics Subject Classifications:** 00A06, 91A80, 91B12, 91B14, 91-02, 91A35.

**Keywords and Phrases:** *Approval Voting, Grading, Majority Judgment, Medium Di erence, Voting Method.*

# 1. Introduction

Votes rank prominently in all countries. Indeed to elect a president of the republic, deputies and mayors are proceeded by votes. According to [9] in many countries (commu-nities, groups, committees), the translation of the democratic ideal takes place by resorting to one version or another of a \majority" method, and that this voting system can lead to surprising results. In the literature, this system is challenged by many theorists of the theory of social choice. This is the case for example in [3] where Michel Balinski and Rida Laraki presented some setbacks of the majority vote.

Similarly, according to [9], the one or two-round majority voting system contains a large number of known and proven defects. Like the majority vote, many other voting methods abound in the literature, but many of them have shortcomings, and therefore do not allow to determine the real will of the voters.

Indeed in [14], it is shown that all systems of voting by classi cation, rating voting systems also generate defects. Sometimes the results of votes lead to huge problems such as popular uprisings, wars and so on. In [14], the way of voting and the current voting system in France are extremely simple but have many aws that can pervert the expres-sion of the popular will.

According to [13] the electoral procedures are very often formalized and studied in an ordinal context where every voter is supposed to be able to classify in order of preference, all the options subject to the collective decision, and that this method is dominant in social choice theory. Long dominated by the votes by classi cation, one of the major concerns turns to the votes by notes. This is the case in [13] where authors question classi cation voting systems and propose as an alternative aggregation methods based on the evaluation principle.

Similarly in [5], some authors reject the ordinal approach of individual preferences. E orts seem to be focusing more and more on searching for a voting system whose result of aggregation operated reflects at best the preferences of the electors. The search for a voting method that best reflects individual preferences is timely.

According to [4], approval voting does not require preferences ordinal. In this system, each voter is free to vote for (approve) the number of candidates he wishes. In addition to its interesting theoretical properties, approval voting o ers electors great exibility in expressing their choices [5] and in [13]. Approval voting, introduced notably by Brams and Fishburn [7, 8] and by Weber [16] , can be regarded as the simplest example of these systems of vote by note. In order to mitigate all these di culties related to the electoral system, in this work, we have combined several methods in order to achieve an adequate voting method. The main purpose of this article is to improve the compensation found when using the arithmetic mean. This method uses both the median and the arithmetic mean and the mean deviation. It also raises \cumulative" or \approval voting".

## 2. State of the art

### 2.1. Definition of Approval Voting

Approval voting is a method with good properties according to the literature. It allows each voter to approve one, two, all candidates or none of them. The elector is not restricted to voting for a single candidate. He may choose or, approve, several candidates, all or none if he wishes but he cannot vote several times for the same candidate. The winner is the candidate who has received the most approvals. This type of ballot, though simple, verifies very interesting properties and shows itself in many points superior to the majority vote [6].

### 2.2. Specific voting properties

According to [15], the desirable properties for a social choice function are:
- Neutrality *(N)*: If each voter reverses his preference, the selected candidate changes too.
- Anonymity *(A)*: If one permutes voters (or even with other voters), the elected candidate does not change.
- Pareto-consistency *(P )*: If all the voters prefer candidate x to candidate y, then x must be the election winner.
- Monotoncity *(M)*: If one or more voters reclassify a candidate x better, then x does not have ultimately to be less better placed in this election.
- Independence of Irrelevant Alternatives *(IIA)*: To classify two candidates among several others, it must be enough to know preferences of each voter for these two candidates. Their choices for others do not influence the classification between these candidates as well as the addition or the withdrawal of a candidate.
- Absence of dictator *(N D)*: The rule should not simply reflect the views of a single and even judge, whatever the circumstances.

- Condorcet Criterion *(CC)*: If a competitor is ranked in front of each of the others competitors by a majority of judges in a one-to-one comparison, it must be placed alone at the top of the final standings.

## 2.3. Description of the Majority Judgment

This description comes from [11, 12]. Balinski and Laraki [1] adopted, in their 2007 experience in the French presidential elections, the following common language:

$$\{Excellent\ (E), Very\ Good\ (VG), Good\ (G), Acceptable\ (A), Poor\ (P), To\ Reject\ (R)\}$$

We call common language a set $\mathcal{L} = \{g_1, g_2, ..., g_k\}$ strictly ordered by " > " such as $g1 > g2 > ... > gk$ ($g_i \geq g_j := g_i > g_j$ or $g_i = g_j$). Note that we can also have a common language be an in nite set such as the interval [0, 1] real numbers with its natural order. Note the possibility for a voter to assign the same assessment to more than two candidates.

As such, a voter may award a candidate $x$ the **VG** score, a candidate $\mathcal{Y}$ the **VG** note and another candidate $\mathcal{Z}$ the note **G**: In the context of Arrow, we will say: "$x$ is at least as good as $\mathcal{Y}$", "$\mathcal{Y}$ is at least as good as $x$ ", "$x$ is at least as good as $\mathcal{Z}$ ", "$\mathcal{Y}$ is at least as good as $\mathcal{Z}$ ", "$x$ is preferred to $\mathcal{Z}$ ", "$\mathcal{Y}$ is preferred to $\mathcal{Z}$", "$x$ is indifferent to $\mathcal{Y}$".

A function $F$ is a it ranking method if it associates to any pro le a single rank [in the same language] for any candidate. So, $F: L^{m \times n} \to L^m$. Where $m$ is the number of candidates, and $n$ the number of judges or voters.

Let $A_i$ be a candidate or competitor with grades $g_{i1}, g_{i2}, ..., g_{in}$ where $g_{i1} \geq g_{i2} \geq ... g_{in}$. Then the majority or majority grade $f^{maj}[A_i]$ is by definition:

$$f^{maj}(A_i) = \begin{cases} f^{\frac{n+1}{2}}, & (g_{i1}, g_{i2}, ..., g_n), \text{if } n \text{ is odd;} \\ f^{\frac{n+2}{2}}, & (g_{i1}, g_{i2}, ..., g_n), \text{if } si\ n \text{ is even.} \end{cases}$$

For example, if 5 judges award grades 4, 8, 7, 9, 5 to $A_i$,

$$f^{maj}(A_i) = f^3(9,8,7,5,4) = 7.$$

And if 8 judges award grades 9, 7, 3, 6, 5, 4, 5, 8 to $A_i$,

$$f^{maj}(A_i) = f^5(9,8,7,6,5,5,4,3) = 5.$$

**Tie-Breaking** (See [1, 2])

When the majority grades of two candidates are different, the one with the highest rank is ranked before the other. The majority ranking $>_{maj}$ between two candidates evaluated by the same jury is determined by a repeated application of the majority rank:

- *If $f^{maj}(A) > f^{maj}(B)$ so $A >_{maj} B$*
- *If $f^{maj}(A) = f^{maj}(B)$* one majority-grade is dropped from the grades of each of the contestants, and the procedure is repeated.

Balinski and Laraki [2] give this example to illustrate their definition:
Suppose $A$ and $B$ are evaluated by a 7 voting jury:

| A | 85 | 73 | 78 | 90 | 69 | 70 | 73 |
|---|----|----|----|----|----|----|----|
| B | 77 | 70 | 95 | 81 | 73 | 73 | 66 |

The ordered profile is:

| A | 90 | 85 | 78 | **73** | 73 | 70 | 69 |
|---|----|----|----|--------|----|----|----|
| B | 95 | 81 | 77 | **73** | 73 | 70 | 69 |

$f_1^{maj}(A) = f_1^{maj}(B) = 73$. By definition, we reject 7 from both lists and we get:

| 90 | 85 | 78 | **73** | 70 | 69 |
|----|----|----|--------|----|----|
| 95 | 81 | 77 | **73** | 70 | 66 |

$f_2^{maj}(A) = f_2^{maj}(B) = 73$. By definition, we reject 7 from both lists and we get:

| A | 90 | 85 | **78** | 70 | 69 |
|---|----|----|--------|----|----|
| B | 95 | 81 | **77** | 70 | 6 |

$f_3^{maj}(A) = 78 > f_3^{maj}(B) = 77$. Since then, $A >_{maj} B$.

It is clear that the majority position always ranks one candidate before the other unless the judges give them the same rank. In case there are several judges or voters (presidential elections for example), Balinski and Laraki present a way of dealing with *tie-break*. The majority of a candidate $f^{maj}(A) = \alpha$ is a triplet $(p_A; \alpha^*; q_A)$ where $p$ is the number or percentage of the candidate's ranks that are greater than the majority rank, $q$ is the number or percentage of the candidate's ranks that are lower than the rank of majority, and $\alpha^* = \alpha^+ \, if \, p > q \, and \, \alpha^* = \alpha^- \, if \, p \leq q$. $\alpha^*$ is called the modifed majority rank of the candidate.

By de nition, $\alpha^* > \beta^*$ if and only if $\alpha > \beta$ or
$(\alpha = \beta \, and \, \alpha^* = \alpha^+ \, and \, \beta^* = \alpha^-)$.

Balinski and Laraki use majority gauge to de ne the majority $-$ gauge $-$ ranking $>_{mg}$. Let $A$ and $B$ two candidates with respective majority gauges $(p_A, \alpha_A^*, q_A)$ and $(p_B, \alpha_B^*, q_B)$. So $A >_{mg} B$ or $(p_A, \alpha_A^*, q_A) >_{mg} (p_B, \alpha_B^*, q_B)$ if and only if $\alpha^* > \beta^*$ or $(\alpha_A^* = \alpha_A^* = \alpha^+ \, and \, p_A > p_B)$ or $(\alpha_A^* = \alpha_A^* = \alpha^- \, and \, p_A < p_B)$.
Manzoor Ahmed Zahid [17, 18] shows that the ranking by majority rule may not decide between candidates in certain cases. A theorem uttered by Balinski and Laraki (Theorem 14.1 in [2]) shows that:

$$A >_{mg} B \implies A >_{maj} B.$$

Zahid then takes an example that illustrates a case where $A >_{mg} B$, but neither $B >_{maj} A$ nor $B >_{mg} A$.

| Candidate | p | Excellent | Very good | Good | Pretty Good | Passable | To Reject | q | Total |
|---|---|---|---|---|---|---|---|---|---|
| A | **5** | 2 | 3 | 3 | 1 | 3 | 3 | 7 | 15 |
| B | **6** | 3 | 3 | 2 | 0 | 2 | 5 | 7 | 15 |

The majority of $A$ is $(5, Good^-, 7)$ and that of $B$ is $(6, Good^-, 7)$. As $q_A = q_B = 7$, the majority rule makes no decision and yet it is easy to check that $A >_{maj} B$.

## 2.4. Vote by rating

This example was designed by ourselves.
Consider a vote of 11 voters and 4 candidates:
Candidate 1: 1 1 1 1 1 1 1 5 5 5 5
Candidate 2: 1 3 3 3 3 3 3 3 3 3 3
Candidate 3: 1 1 1 1 1 5 5 5 5 5 5
Candidate 4: 1 2 2 2 2 3 3 3 3 3 3
Candidate 5:1 1 1 1 1 1 5 5 5 5 5
Candidate 6:1 1 1 2 4 4 4 4 4 5 5

Using the arithmetic mean we nd: On the one hand candidates 1 and candidate 4 each have 27 points; But most of the majority does not want the candidate 1 to be elected.

On the other hand candidates 2 and candidate 5 each have 31 points. It is also noted that candidate 2 is better liked than candidate 5. Candidates 3 and 6 also have the same number of points, but candidate 6 seems more than candidate 3. It is summarized in the following table:

| | $c_1$ | $c_2$ | $c_3$ | $c_4$ | $c_5$ | $c_6$ |
|---|---|---|---|---|---|---|
| $x_1$ | 1 | 1 | 1 | 1 | 1 | 1 |
| $x_2$ | 1 | 3 | 1 | 2 | 1 | 1 |
| $x_3$ | 1 | 3 | 1 | 2 | 1 | 1 |
| $x_4$ | 1 | 3 | 1 | 2 | 1 | 2 |
| $x_5$ | 1 | 3 | 1 | 2 | 1 | 4 |
| $x_6$ | 1 | 3 | 5 | 3 | 1 | 4 |
| $x_7$ | 1 | 3 | 5 | 3 | 5 | 4 |
| $x_8$ | 5 | 3 | 5 | 3 | 5 | 4 |
| $x_9$ | 5 | 3 | 5 | 3 | 5 | 4 |
| $x_{10}$ | 5 | 3 | 5 | 3 | 5 | 5 |
| $x_{11}$ | 5 | 3 | 5 | 3 | 5 | 5 |
| $\bar{x}$ | 2.45 | 2.81 | 3.18 | 2.45 | 2.81 | 3.18 |

## 2.5. Ranking vote

These examples are taken from [9].

**Example 1.** *Let $\{a, b, c \ldots, z\}$ be an example of 26 candidates for which there are 100 voters whose preferences are as follows:*
*51 voters have preference $a \succ b \succ c \succ \ldots y \succ z$*
*49 voters have preference $z \succ b \succ c \succ \ldots y \succ a$.*

**Example 2.** *Let $\{a, b, c\}$ be the set of all candidates in an election involving 21 voters whose preferences are as follows: 10 voters have preferences $a \succ b \succ c$*
*6 voters have preferences $b \succ c \succ a$*
*5 voters have preferences $c \succ b \succ a$.*

**Example 3.** *Let $\{a, b, c, d\}$ be all candidates in an election involving 21 voters whose preferences are as follows: 10 voters have preferences $b \succ a \succ c \succ d$*
*6 voters have preferences $c \succ a \succ d \succ b$*
*5 voters have preferences $a \succ d \succ b \succ c$.*

In example 1, under the assumption of the sincerity of the voters, the candidate will receive 51 votes against 49 for the candidate z. The other candidates do not receive any votes; the candidate is elected by absolute majority. But the elected candidate is badly perceived by a large proportion of the voters whereas the candidate b could constitute "a good compromise".

In example 2, under the hypothesis of the sincerity of voters the candidate will receive 10 votes against 6 and 5 respectively for candidates $b$ and $c$. The candidate is elected with 10 votes out of 21. This re ects little the wishes of the majority of voters. It is noted, however, that an absolute majority prefers all other candidates to the one elected (11 voters out of 21 prefer $b$ and $c$ to $a$).

In example 3, in the French system, only candidates $b$ and $c$ remain in the running for the second round, and $b$ win with 15/21, although an absolute majority (11/21) of voters prefers both candidate $a$ and candidate $d$.

## 2.6. Problematic

The conclusion that emerges is that at the general level, many voting methods generate paradoxes. According to [11], Majority Judgment may produce controversial results in some cases. According to [2], majority voting is a poor measure of opinion. Why? He forces the elector to vote for a single candidate, while he has much more nuanced opinions on all. Some might support several; others do not like the candidate for whom they voted; still others make the strategic choice of the least bad among those whom they consider to have a chance. Nevertheless, each vote is interpreted as a membership and is worth "1". So, the sum of votes that are totally different in sense determines the result. It is not surprising that the induced political weight is far from reality.

According to [5], the two-round majority vote suffers from several defaults. It does not meet Condorcet's criterion that a candidate who beats all his competitors in majority duels must be elected. It encourages strategic voting and does not encourage participation in the sense that some voters may have an interest in not to vote. According to [13] classification voting systems use ordinal preferences voters and that this ordinal context does not make it possible to judge (or appreciate) the different options independently. According to [14], the one or two-round majority voting system has a large number of widely known and proven defects.

We also found through our example on vote by grading that the aggregation using the arithmetic mean gives controversial results. It is in this context that we will try through this article to find a new method, with the main concern that this one result in results with little contrast. A method that avoids Borda's paradox that a candidate can be elected while he has against him a majority of voters.

## 3. Voting system based on average deviation assessments

### 3.1. Description

The method consists of classifying candidates into five classes in order of preference. A candidate ranked in the best class gets 5 points. If he is ranked in the one following the first, he gets 4, and so on until the last of the classes where he gets 1 point. The next phase is to order a candidate's notes in ascending order. The median of the series is then determined. If the median score of a candidate is 1 or 1.5 depending on whether the number of voters is even or odd, then it is automatically eliminated.

In other cases, the arithmetic mean and the mean deviation are calculated. Of course, the candidate with the best average and the smallest average difference is elected. In case of a tie, the process is repeated.

So let us consider a $E$ set of m candidates for an election, with $m \geq 2$, that is to say $E = \{c_1, c_2, ..., c_m\}$ and $F$ a set of voters with $s \geq 2$, that is to say $F = \{v_1, v_2, ..., v_s\}$. So the method is as follows:

- Each of the $s$ voters uses $P(E)$ items that are disjoint and whose meeting gives $E$, according to the following order: choice 1, choice 2, choice 3, choice 4, choice 5.
- It assigns each element of each of its subsets respectively the note 1, 2, 3, 4, 5. Example: Let $E = \{c_1, c_2, c_3, c_4, c_5\}$ be a set of 5 candidates. The following table represents the choice of a voter:

| $\{c_1\}$ | $\{c_2\}$ | $\{c_3\}$ | $\{c_4\}$ | $\{c_5\}$ |
|---|---|---|---|---|

Let us now calculate the absolute average difference between the scores of the different candidates. Note that in this table, we also calculated the average deviation of candidate 1, this is optional because the median score of the latter is 1. And according to the method the candidate 1 is automatically eliminated.

| Candidate 1 | | | | | | | | | | | | |
|---|---|---|---|---|---|---|---|---|---|---|---|---|
| $x_1$ | 1 | 1 | 1 | 1 | 1 | 1 | 1 | 5 | 5 | 5 | 5 | $E_m$ |
| $|x_i - \bar{x}|$ | 1.45 | 1.45 | 1.45 | 1.45 | 1.45 | 1.45 | 1.45 | 2.55 | 2.55 | 2.55 | 2.55 | **1.85** |

| Candidate 2 | | | | | | | | | | | | |
|---|---|---|---|---|---|---|---|---|---|---|---|---|
| $x_1$ | 1 | 3 | 3 | 3 | 3 | 3 | 3 | 3 | 3 | 3 | 3 | $E_m$ |
| $|x_i - \bar{x}|$ | 1.81 | 0.19 | 0.19 | 0.19 | 0.19 | 0.19 | 0.19 | 0.19 | 0.19 | 0.19 | 0.19 | **0.33** |

| Candidate 3 | | | | | | | | | | | | |
|---|---|---|---|---|---|---|---|---|---|---|---|---|
| $x_1$ | 1 | 1 | 1 | 1 | 1 | 5 | 5 | 5 | 5 | 5 | 5 | $E_m$ |
| $|x_i - \bar{x}|$ | 2.18 | 2.18 | 2.18 | 2.18 | 2.18 | 1.82 | 1.82 | 1.82 | 1.82 | 1.82 | 1.82 | **1.98** |

| Candidate 4 | | | | | | | | | | | | |
|---|---|---|---|---|---|---|---|---|---|---|---|---|
| $x_1$ | 1 | 2 | 2 | 2 | 2 | 3 | 3 | 3 | 3 | 3 | 3 | $E_m$ |
| $|x_i - \bar{x}|$ | 1.45 | 0.45 | 0.45 | 0.45 | 0.45 | 0.55 | 0.55 | 0.55 | 0.55 | 0.55 | 0.55 | **0.57** |

| Candidate 5 | | | | | | | | | | | | |
|---|---|---|---|---|---|---|---|---|---|---|---|---|
| $x_1$ | 1 | 1 | 1 | 1 | 1 | 1 | 5 | 5 | 5 | 5 | 5 | $E_m$ |
| $|x_i - \bar{x}|$ | 1.81 | 1.81 | 1.81 | 1.81 | 1.81 | 1.81 | 2.19 | 2.19 | 2.19 | 2.19 | 2.19 | **1.98** |

| Candidate 5 | | | | | | | | | | | | |
|---|---|---|---|---|---|---|---|---|---|---|---|---|
| $x_1$ | 1 | 1 | 1 | 2 | 4 | 4 | 4 | 4 | 4 | 5 | 5 | $E_m$ |
| $|x_i - \bar{x}|$ | 2.18 | 2.18 | 2.18 | 1.18 | 0.82 | 0.82 | 0.82 | 0.82 | 0.82 | 0.82 | 0.82 | **1.47** |

## 3.2. Theorem

The new voting method has the following properties:

(i) It verifies the condorcet criterion.

(ii) The binary actions are independent: To classify for example 2 candidates among several others, it is enough to know the preferences of each voter for these two candidates; their choices for the others do not change the classification between these two candidates.

(iii) Monotony; if one or more voters better reclassify a candidate $x$, then x must not, ultimately be less placed in this election. In other words, if $x$ is elected in a first election and in a second, a voter who has voted against $x$ changes his mind in favor of $x$, then $x$ is still elected.

(iv) Unanimity or pareto.

## 3.3. Proof

(i)     It checks the condorcet criterion: If a candidate beats everyone else at all duels, then x is the winner.

(ii)     The binary actions are independent: to classify for example two candidates among several others, it is enough to know the preferences of each voter for these two candidates; their choices for the others do not change the classification between these two candidates. The calculation of the average and the average difference of these two candidates does not depend on the marks obtained by the other candidates.

(iii)     It is monotonous: in a second election, if an elector who was not for the x candidate first elected, changes his position, the average of x increases and x is still elected.

(iv)     Pareto is trivial.

## 4. Discussion and Perspectives

Voting methods play a vital role in any society. They seem to be involved in the stability of a country. Indeed a voting system leading to a consensus generates less post-election contestation. Votes by ratings that seem better than ratings by theory of choice theorists, present some difficulties. In this article, we found that by only being satisfied with the cumulative points, different candidates, you can elect a candidate who does not reflect a consensus.

We have also, combined the assent voting at the median, the average and the average deviation to determine the new voting mode. Voting by assent is well appreciated in the literature because it fulfills some good properties [6].

Using the median eliminates candidates who are not at all liked by at least (50%) of voters.

Which is an advantage in ballot counting because we do not waste time calculating the mean and the average deviation of the candidates downgraded.

In addition to the combination used gave birth to a voting method with good proper-ties and to have a good compromise, despite some limitations it could generate. Because according to [10], we know since the 1970s, thanks to the work of Gibbard and Satterth-waite that any democratic voting procedure is manipulable: thus, one can never be sure that a voter has revealed his sincere preference, or that he has revealed a false preference, in order to favor the election of a candidate who is better placed strategically.

Our method fulfills many good properties certainly, but is it practicable in terms of optimization of calculations and monetary, because it seems that the average difference is easy to calculate and simple to interpret that unfortunately, it is not provided by most statistical software.

In addition to this, does the method allow to reduce conflicts with those who still refuse to lose votes despite the results provided by the ballot boxes?

Will future research allow us to study the complexity of the new voting system and apply it to the group decision, to solve multi-criteria with several decision makers problem?

# REFERENCES

**[1]** M. Balinski and R. Laraki. A theory of measuring, electing, and ranking. PNAS, 104(21), 2007.

**[2]** M. Balinski and R. Laraki. Majority judgment : measuring, ranking and electing. Technical report, MIT Press, 2010.

**[3]** M. Balinski and R. Laraki. Jugement majoritaire vs vote majoritaire (via les prsidentielles 2011-2012). Cahier no 2012-37, CNRS, 2012.

**[4]** N. Barrot. Sur les aspects computationels du vote par approbation. PhD thesis, Universit Paris-Dauphine, LAMSADE, 2016.

**[5]** A. Baujard and H. Igersheim. Experimentation du vote par note et du vote par approbation lors de l'election presidentielle franaise du 22 avril 2007. Technical report, Centre d'analyse stratgique, 2007.

**[6]** P. Blanchenay. Paradoxes de vote et modes de scrutin en france. Master's thesis, Ecole des Hautes Etudes Commerciales Majeure Economie., 2004.

**[7]** S. J. Brams and P. C. Fishburn. Approval Voting. Birkuser, Cambridge, 1983.

**[8]** S. J. Brams and P. C. Fishburn. Approval Voting. Springer Science, 2nd edition, 2007.

**[9]** D. Bouyssou; T. Marchant and P. Perny. Theorie du choix social et aide multicritere la dcision. Working Paper, LAMSADE, 2005.

**[10]** V. Merlin. La theorie des choix collectifs portee de tous! Commentaires sur quatre livres de vulgarisation de Donald Saari. Mathematiques et Sciences Humaines, 163, 2003.

**[11]** R.-B. M. Ngoie; Z. Savadogo and B. E.-L. Ulungu. Median and average as tools for measuring, electing and Ranking : new propects. Fundamental Journal of Mathemat-ics and Mathematical Sciences, 1(1):9 { 30, 2014.

[12]  R.-B. M. Ngoie; Z. Savadogo and B. E.-L. Ulungu. New prospect in Social Choice Theory : Median and average as tools for measuring, electing and ranking. Advanced Studies in Contemporary Mathematics, 25(1):19 { 38, 2015.

[13]  H. Smaoui and D. Lepelley. Le systeme de vote trois niveaux: Etude d'un nouveau mode de scrutin. Revue d'economie politique, 123(6):827 { 850, 2013.

[14]  J. G. Suitt; A. Guyon; T. Hennion; R. Laraki; X. Starklo ; S. Thibault and B. Favreau. Vers un systme de vote plus juste. Cahier no 2014-20, CNRS, septembre 2014.

[15]  M. Truchon. Choix social et comites de selection: le cas du patinage artistique. ~ Universit Laval, CIRANO, Novembre 2002.

[16]  R. J. Weber. Approval voting. Journal of Economic Perspectives, 9(1):39{49, 1995.

[17]  M. A. Zahid. Majority judgment and pardoxical results. International Journal of Arts and Sciences, 4(20):121 { 131, 2009.

[18]  M. A. Zahid. A new framework for elections. PhD thcsis, Tilburg University., 2012.